Mumblings and Musings

Ayden Gabryel Ryan M. H.

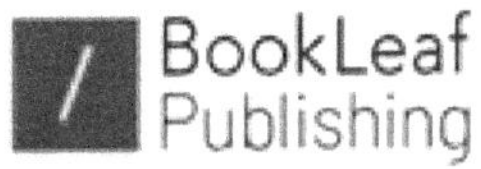

BookLeaf
Publishing

Mumblings and Musings © 2022 Ayden Gabryel Ryan M. H.

All rights reserved.

No part of this publication may be reproduced, stored in a retrieval system, or transmitted, in any form or by any means, electronic, mechanical, photocopying, recording or otherwise, without the prior written permission of the presenters.

Ayden Gabryel Ryan M. H. asserts the moral right to be identified as author of this work.

Presentation by *BookLeaf Publishing*

Web: www.bookleafpub.com

E-mail: info@bookleafpub.com

ISBN: 9789357210690

First edition 2022

DEDICATION

This book is dedicated to my younger self. And to my sister, Cassie, who would have loved to read it.

ACKNOWLEDGEMENT

I'd like to thank my dad, George, for helping make this book happen. And for all the other times he's helped me in the past. And my mom, who's always inspired me to keep creating, and continues to inspire me to this day. I'd like to thank my all of my siblings, but specifically Cassie, Brenden, Jonny, and Violet, who've always lovingly bullied me into getting my shit together. And lastly, my close friends Claudia, Roman, Alex, Megan, Ryan, Tani, Quasar, and to every other friend I didnt name here, for loving me for me, in all of my goofy depressed glory! I love you all so much!

PREFACE

A lot of these poems are sad. Some are more hopeful, and some are just plain silly. I write poems that are sad the best, because I'm generally sad about a lot of things, including but not limited to: van gogh, existing, dropping something, the current state of the world, the fact that all my succulents died, you get the idea. Anyways, maybe watch your favorite kids show after reading this. Just to cheer you up a bit. Happy reading!

Golden Child

I haven't felt like a person.
Not for a while.
Not since I stopped being
Your perfect golden child.

Why do I need expectations to function?

Why do I feel like I'm failing because no one
expects much of me?

Why do I need to feel pressured into being good
at something?
At anything. At everything.

Why am I not good at everything?

Why am I not your perfect, golden child?

Not Sad

I am sad like the last snow to fall
I am sad like paint faded on a wall
Not deeply
Not profound
But in the way you search
For something that can't be found.

It lurks and it creeps
Into my being it seeps
Not sadness, not quite
Just loneliness
And listlessness
And emptiness at night.

I am not sad
I'm not in despair
Some days I just can't tell
If I'm even there
I keep searching for myself
But I can't seem to be found.

If Highschool Finals Make Me Vomit, What Will College Do? (Fuck It.)

From time to time I wonder if

Under certain circumstances I could

Convince the stars to change my trajectory and

Keep me in this bubble of "stressed but not alone"

I'm not ready
To be alone.

Infintesimal

Sometimes I feel small
Like a single speck of sand in the vastness of the
universe
Like a speck of cosmic dust blowing in the solar
wind.

Then I remember, to a microorganism
a grain of sand is giant, a speck of dust a whole
planet.

I am both small and giant, at all times.
Never small enough to not matter
Never big enough to not care

Infinitely Infinitesimal
Endlessly growing and shrinking into myself.

Too much, Too little.

Too much, too little.
Never enough time and never enough to do.
I'm restless and rushed.
There is no middle ground.
No moment where I feel I can rest.

I need a nap, and 20 more tasks to keep me
interested.
I need a coffee, and 20 more minutes to myself.

I'm constantly chasing,
Something to do,
Nothing to do.
Something to be.

I want to be something.
Do I have to do something to be?

I think therefore I am doesn't work for me,
because often I think I'm not.

I'm not. I am. I could be, if I did more.

I wouldn't be if I did too much, not enough.

Too much, too little.
I feel both often.

I'm too much.
I'm too little.
I'm not doing enough.
I'm doing too much.

I'm doing too much.

Little Wonders

Life is in the little wonders, I think.
In birdsong, and sun beams
In a bubbling creak
The crunch of leaves on a fall day
In a smile
A hug
A handshake
Highfives and fist bumps
In sharing a laugh over something mundane
In inside jokes and stupid meme.
In flowers blooming
In blush on cheeks
In little glances
In the squeak of a mouse you can't see.
Life is in the little wonders, I think.

5 days

When I started this book
I thought it'd be a breeze
But now I have only five days
To finish the rest of these.

God I wish I didnt procrastinate.

Cassie

I promise, sister, to go on even if it hurts without you.
I promise, to laugh in spite of the pain.
I promise, to carry you with me for the rest of my days.
And spread the love, the joy, the hope you gave me.
I promise, sister, I won't give up.
Even on days when everything feels like too much.
I promise to remember you, in everything I do.
I promise, sister, I wont forget everything you taught me.
I promise to pass it along, to friends and family and strangers alike.
I promise to share your light in your absence.
I promise when I see you again, you'll be able to say you're proud.
Even though I know you already are.
I promise, sister.

Home

Is home where the heart is?
Or is it where you can sleep at night?
Is it the feeling of comfort you get from being
truly known and accepted still?
Is it in the arms of your dearest friend?
Is it being surrounded by light and laughter and
beauty?
Is it deep in the woods, where theres nothing to
hear but birds?
Tucked away in a cave, with bats flitting
overhead?
Maybe home isn't a place at all.
But a feeling.
Belonging, being known, being loved for all
your little flaws.
I think thats home to me.

Static

Lately, any time I try to write all I get is static.
My head is buzzing too quickly for me to grab
onto a thought and drag it into words.
I wish it would slow, some days.
Most days, honestly.

Scars

My knees are scarred from a bicycle accident I
took as a child.
I flipped my bike onto asphalt, and scraped my
knees up so bad there were rocks stuck in them.
I have two pencil lead scars.
One on my arm and one on the side of my knee,
from first and second grade, respectively.
I have a scar on my stomach from a spider bite I
got living in a 130 year old house.
My brothers tell me it got really gross, but I
don't remember this.
Maybe its because I blocked it out?
I still don't know.
I have scars on my thighs, from painful times in
my life.
These ones are the ones that hurt the most.
I have a scar on my hand from a knife I used to
cut eggplant in FCS.
We were making ratatouille, I think.
I have a scar on the very tip of my ring finger.
I got that one while cutting up dandelions with
pruning shears when I was nine.
The hospital super glued it back on.
I have many scars, some bigger but most small,
some visible and others long faded.

I used to hate a lot of them.
But now I'm growing to love them.
They show my journey, my life.
And they show that I've survived it all.
And I will continue to survive.
For myself, and no one else.

A poem to myself

Grow up, but don't lose your child like wonder.
Stop being a pushover, but don't lose your
helpfulness.
Stop caring so much about what others think.
Stop overthinking everything.
Stop questioning yourself.
Start loving yourself.
Start sleeping enough.
Start eating better, and work out more.
Get better at saving money, and find hobbies you
enjoy.
Remember that no one expects perfection.
Remember that you are loved, and stop
questioning the love you are given.
Remember that no one is judging you, and if
they are who gives a fuck.
Keep smiling through the bad
Keep showing your heart on your sleeve.
Keep believing in yourself.
Keep on fighting, no matter how the odds are
stacked against you.
Keep growing, and forget the notion that you
need acknowledgement for your growth.
Take care of yourself.
Take care of a plant (you can do it this time!)

Take care of your friends, but don't extend so
much help that you lose yourself.
Take photos of the things you love, and post
them!
Give yourself a break and know that growth isn't
linear.
Know that everything will be okay, and you will
make it through.
Don't worry about being the besr version of
yourself, but your favorite version of yourself.
Learn how to take criticism.
Learn how to take advice.
Learn how to take compliments.
Learn how to talk about the things you need.
Learn how to set boundaries.
Learn how to drive a car, maybe.
Learn to love yourself for every piece of
yourself, no matter how bruised, broken, or
scarred.
Love fiercely, whole heartedly, freely.
You will be okay.

Beads

I got angry, the other night.
Unreasonably so, considering the situation.

It had been building, for a while.
And I'm not good at letting it out.

So I threw a box of mine.
It was made of plastic.
And it held my bracelets, and earrings, and other things.

And I threw it at the door.
The whole thing shattered.

The noise almost brought me peace, for a second.
In the same way shattering glass does.

Maybe I need to go to one of those places where you just get to break things.
That'd be a good way to get out my anger I suppose.

But then I noticed beads.

Scattered across the floor from the point of
impact.

Tigers eye and turquoise.
Two bracelets of mine had broken when I threw
the box.

Fortunately, I found all of the pieces.
And I have elastic string so I can put them back
together.

Like I will put myself back together.
With elastic string and glue.

I will hold myself back together until I am
whole.
Until it no longer hurts to be.

Until I am no longer throwing myself to the
floor.
Snapping, and splitting myself apart.

I will string myself back together.
And though I won't be the same, I will still be
me.

Made of tigers eye and turquoise.
I will be whole again.

Forgetful

I had an idea for a poem, I swear I did.

It was going to be beautiful, moving, inspiring even!

I had it and then-

Then I opened the page and-

And well I still needed to write my acknowledgement, and preface, and well...

I forgot it.
I got focused on those things and it slipped away.

So instead I'm writing this poem about forgetting it.

I'm glad I didnt forget this one too, or else this book'd have no more poems in it!

Universe

I think about the universe a lot.
About the vastness of it.

Its a never ending, seemingly uncaring being.
And it must be conscious, for there are parts of it
that are.

We are conscious, and part of the universe.

It makes me think of how uncaring it really is.
Or isn't, I suppose.

If the universe were uncaring, wed never have
existed to experience what we have.
If the universe were uncaring we'd never know
happiness, or love.

If the universe were uncaring it would have
given us none of those things.

Even if they were all it gave us under the
intention of caring, we'd never know what it was
to experience it.

If all you had was light, you'd never know the
difference between it and darkness.

Happiness cannot exist without sadness.
We wouldn't recognize it if it did.

The universe gave us balance.
It wouldn't have if it were uncaring.

It wouldn't have given us billions of stars to
inspire us to go beyond our world.
It wouldn't have given us nature to inspire us to
care for the world.
It wouldn't have given us each other, to know
and to love.

The universe cares, or at least I think it does.
It must, for all that its given us.

Night

I like being awake at night.

When the world is silent and the moon keeps watch over the world.

I gaze at the stars and feel more at home than ever.

Searching

I think I've lost a piece of myself.

In middle school hallways.
Or the homes I used to live in.

Its scattered throughout the places I have been.
Waiting in the places I have yet to go.

Im looking for this piece of me.
The one thing that finally clicks.

When I look at what I'm doing and think that
this...
This must be my purpose.

I'm waiting for my calling to find me.
But maybe its time for me to start searching.

Love

I love too deeply sometimes.
I go all in on something that will only end in
pain.
Even when I know it will end in flames.

But I think its also lovely.
How I am able to freely give all of my heart to
someone.
No matter how badly it has been bruised in the
past.

My heart is not shattered.

Of course I'm sad about the loss, and the hurt.

But it teaches me who I am.
Who I want.
What I can and can't put up with.

So I choose not to regret the past, when I have
loved too deeply.
I choose to continue loving with my whole heart.

Instead of locking it away, hiding that part of
myself.

I'd rather feel alive than hidden.

Rising

The sun may fall every night
Leave the world bathed in darkness.

But like clockwork she always returns.
Brings beauty into the world in the form of a sun
rise.

No matter how many times she falls.
She claws her way back up to us.

No matter how many times I fall.
I will claw my way back up.

I will be my own sun.

Change

I wish I could change.
Stretch my body into something more.

A winged beast, perhaps.
Soaring free above the clouds.

Or maybe a sea-faring creature.
Endlessly exploring the depths.

I want to be so much more than human.

Goodbye

Sadness has visited and left.
Happiness must get home before its too late.
Anger has stormed off again.
And anxiety is still deciding whether or not to
come.

Poems have said their piece and ended.
Stories are on the road to find more.
And though this is a goodbye.
I'll walk you to the door.

I'll wave as you leave, and hope for your safe
return.
Thank you for coming
And thank you for leaving.

Thank you for being.
Thank you, for saying goodbye.

www.ingramcontent.com/pod-product-compliance
Lightning Source LLC
La Vergne TN
LVHW021332200726
843509LV00014B/2500